Hill M

1836 Brookdale Rd.

Naperville, IL 60563

PEARL HARBOR!

by

Wallace B. Black
and
Jean F. Blashfield

CRESTWOOD HOUSE
New York

Collier Macmillan Canada
Toronto

Maxwell Macmillan International Publishing Group
New York Oxford Singapore Sydney

Library of Congress Cataloging-in-Publication Data

Black, Wallace B.
   Pearl Harbor! / by Wallace B. Black and Jean F. Blashfield. – 1st ed.
      p.   cm. – (World War II 50th anniversary series)
   Includes index.
   Summary: Details the anatomy of the shocking raid on the U.S. Navy's Pacific fleet that put America at war with Japan. Recounts Japanese strategy and tactics, and focuses on the reasons for the Americans' surprise.
   ISBN 0-89686-555-X
   1. Pearl Harbor (Hawaii), Attack on, 1941 – Juvenile literature.
[1. Pearl Harbor (Hawaii), Attack on, 1941. 2. World War, 1939-1945 – Causes.]
I. Blashfield, Jean F. II. Title. III. Series: Black, Wallace B. World War II
50th anniversary series.
D767.92.B53 1991
940.54'26–dc20

                                                        90-45621
                                                           CIP
                                                            AC

Created and produced by B&B Publishing Inc.

Picture Credits

Imperial War Museum - pages 41, 44 (top, center left)
National Archives - pages 4, 5, 6 12, 14, 19, 24-25, 32, 33 (bottom), 35, 37, 45 (all)
United States Air Force - page 44 (center right)
United States Navy - pages 3, 8, 9, 16, 20, 21, 22, 23, 27, 28, 29, 30, 31, 33 (top), 34, 36, 38, 40, 41,
   42, 44 (bottom)
Steve Sullivan - Maps - pages 17, 43

CRESTWOOD   Macmillan Publishing Company   Collier Macmillan Canada, Inc.
HOUSE   866 Third Avenue   1200 Eglinton Avenue East
                  New York, NY 10022   Suite 200
                                                   Don Mills, Ontario M3C 3N1

Printed in the United States of America

First Edition

10 9 8 7 6 5 4 3 2 1

CONTENTS

Chapter 1

PEARL HARBOR SLEEPS

The sun had risen slowly out of the Pacific Ocean east of Hawaii. All was quiet and peaceful. Those beautiful islands had belonged to the United States since 1898. The huge, natural harbor at Pearl Harbor was just a few miles from the big city of Honolulu on the island of Oahu. It had been used by the U.S. Navy since 1887.

Following orders, many ships of the Pacific Fleet of the U.S. Navy returned to Pearl Harbor each weekend for rest and recreation. On Sunday morning, December 7, 1941, there were 94 ships in the harbor. Some were tied up to the docks at Ford Island in the center of the harbor. Others were being repaired in huge dry docks. Still other ships floated peacefully at anchor.

A beautiful view of the big, natural harbor on the island of Oahu

Japan had been making warlike threats for some time. The Hawaiian military forces should have been on active alert around the clock, seven days a week. Instead, that Sunday morning, the ships' boilers were cold. Only a few crew members were on duty. All the others were getting ready for usual peacetime weekend activities. Returning to port each weekend was good for morale, according to the navy commander, Admiral Husband E. Kimmel. He saw no reason to keep the fleet at sea on weekends.

At home in the States, Americans were also enjoying a quiet, peaceful Sunday. Except for a few well-informed people, thoughts of war were far from everyone's mind.

But that morning, before the citizens and soldiers and sailors of Hawaii awoke, strange things were happening. Under cover of darkness, a 33-ship Japanese strike force was steaming across the Pacific Ocean, heading for the Hawaiian Islands. When they neared, about 200 miles to the north, Japanese aircraft carriers launched a huge force of fighters and bombers. At 7:55 A.M. on Sunday, December 7, 1941, Pearl Harbor was attacked.

Admiral Kimmel (center) *and his staff at work before Pearl Harbor*

Without warning, Japanese aircraft bombed the harbor and the military bases on the island of Oahu. One day later, President Franklin D. Roosevelt described December 7 as "a date which will live in infamy."

War had been threatening for some time. Like Germany, Japan had been on the march for several years. The Japanese wanted more space and more natural resources. They were already fighting and taking over parts of China.

America had watched Japan's expansion with concern. President Roosevelt finally asked Japan to stop its warlike advances. U.S. trade with Japan was forbidden.

The Japanese said that they would stop their activities if the United States would restore normal trade. After many months of meetings, the two countries were still arguing.

U.S. naval intelligence officers had broken the code used by the Japanese to send secret messages. Some messages had been intercepted. The United States knew that Japan was preparing to go to war. But no one thought it would be against the United States.

Too Late

At 9 A.M. in Washington, D.C. (4 o'clock in the morning in Hawaii), on December 7, another secret message was intercepted by the navy. The message from the Japanese government in Tokyo told Ambassador Kichisaburo Nomura to reject all U.S. demands. He was told to deliver the message to Secretary of State Cordell Hull at 1:00 P.M. Washington time. (This would be just after the attack on Pearl Harbor had started.)

Reading the message, the naval intelligence officers in Washington became worried. They tried to contact the White House but could not. They also could not contact General George C. Marshall, the army chief of staff. He was out on his regular Sunday-morning horseback ride.

When General Marshall was finally reached, it was

A U.S. Navy Catalina PBY patrol bomber taking off

already 6:30 in Hawaii. He sent a message to U.S. military commanders in Hawaii and the Philippines. The message said that war might break out at any time. No notice of a possible attack on U.S. bases was given. But even if this advice had been given, the message was not delivered in Hawaii until long after the Japanese attack had begun.

WARNING 1:
Submarine Sighted near Pearl Harbor

At 4:00 A.M. on the morning of December 7, the American minesweeper USS *Condor* was on patrol outside the entrance to Pearl Harbor. It was usually dull duty. But that morning an excited young officer reported sighting an unidentified submarine. Two destroyers were called to help search. They failed to find the submarine.

Two hours later, the pilot of a Catalina PBY patrol bomber also reported seeing an unidentified submarine. One destroyer then spotted a Japanese midget submarine outside the entrance to Pearl Harbor. Its deck guns fired and sank the sub. A few minutes later sailors on the destroyers spotted another sub. The Catalina bomber dropped depth charges for another possible kill.

Unknown to the U.S. command, Japanese two-man midget submarines had been towed to Hawaii by larger Japanese submarines. They had been ordered to enter Pearl Harbor and attack the ships anchored there.

Told of the submarine sightings, Admiral Kimmel did not believe that a major attack was about to take place. He probably thought the submarines were just spying on U.S. Navy activities. Few people believed that the Japanese would sail 4,000 miles to attack Pearl Harbor.

A Japanese midget submarine that was damaged by depth charges

WARNING 2:
Unidentified Aircraft

On the northern tip of Oahu island, army privates Joe Lockard and George Elliott were on duty at a new radar station. Radar had recently been developed. The equipment sent out radio waves that bounced off aircraft in flight. The returning signals showed distance, altitude, direction of flight, and speed of approaching aircraft.

Both Lockard and Elliott were new to their jobs. All they usually saw was a blank screen. Suddenly, at 7:02 A.M. that morning, they noticed a large "blip" of light on the screen. This bright blip meant that a group of aircraft was coming in from the north. The aircraft were about 130 miles away at an altitude of 5,000 feet. They were approaching Oahu at about 165 miles per hour.

Excited, Private Lockard called the air-warning center on the island to report the sighting. The officer on duty there was not worried. He thought that the blip showed planes returning from U.S. aircraft carriers or perhaps a flight of B-17 bombers arriving from California. He did not tell anyone else about the sighting.

No longer bored, Lockard and Elliott watched the blip grow larger. The approaching aircraft finally disappeared from the radar screen as they swept in behind a range of hills. The two men then heard explosions as Japanese bombs began to fall on Pearl Harbor.

Even if they had been taken seriously, these two warnings would have been of no help. The battleships in the harbor would not have been able to start up and move out to sea. Only a few aircraft could have been armed and taken off in time to intercept the raiders. A great Japanese victory was certain.

CHAPTER 2

JAPAN PREPARES FOR WAR

Japan had begun to prepare for its conquest of Asia as early as 1931. The world was in a deep economic depression. Japan's industries were in trouble. Over 60 million people were crowded on Japan's tiny islands. The Japanese were suffering. They needed more living space. They needed more food and more raw materials.

Emperor Hirohito receiving the war proclamation from Japan's prime minister, General Hideki Tojo

Crack Japanese troops take over more territory in northeast China.

Emperor Hirohito was the supreme ruler of Japan. But control was in the hands of the nation's military leaders and the Japanese cabinet. These high-ranking civilian and military officials were looking for answers to Japan's problems. The answers they found led the country to war.

Japan was jealous of the British because they controlled rubber, tin and other raw materials found in India, Burma and Malaya. Japan wanted the rubber plantations in French Indochina. They wanted the oil wells of Dutch-controlled Indonesia. The Japanese leaders also wanted the lands and resources of their huge neighbor, China.

They planned to drive out all the Europeans who had set up colonies in Asia. The Japanese would then take control of all China and Southeast Asia.

Taking Over Asia

Japan began its first military action on the continent of Asia in 1931. The Japanese invaded Manchuria, a region in northeastern China. Year after year they took over more territory until war with China broke out in 1937.

Within a few years Japan held most of the eastern half of China. It controlled most of China's transportation, seaports and industrial cities. Generalissimo Chiang Kai-shek had become supreme commander of the Chinese government. But even with help from the Soviet Union, Italy and the U.S., the Chinese army could not stop the Japanese advance.

Japan's well-trained armies continued to slaughter Chinese soldiers and civilians. They captured more Chinese cities. The Japanese navy began building the biggest battleships and aircraft carriers in the world. They planned to control all of Asia. Japan was rapidly becoming a great military power. And, as in Germany, the people in the Japanese government did not care how cruel they had to be to other people to win.

America Gets Involved

The United States sent armed gunboats to China to protect U.S. citizens. On December 12, 1937, the Japanese deliberately bombed and sank the USS *Panay* in the Yangtze River. But most Americans didn't care. They were more concerned with the problems of the Great Depression. And they thought the boat shouldn't have been there in the first place. They wanted no part in a war with nations half a world away.

President Roosevelt wanted to stop Japan. In 1939 he ordered the U.S. Pacific Fleet to be stationed at Pearl Harbor in Hawaii as a warning. In 1940 he called for American

Japanese artillery and aircraft bombarded Chinese cities without mercy.

industry to stop furnishing oil, steel and materials of war to Japan. These actions slowed the Japanese military in Asia. Japanese leaders, however, were even more determined to continue their advances.

Germany was invading country after country in Europe. Dutch, French and British armed forces were needed there. The colonies had to take care of themselves. Japan declared itself neutral in the European war. However, as soon as France surrendered to the Nazis, the Japanese occupied French Indochina (now Vietnam). They also forced the Dutch colonies in Sumatra and Indonesia to provide Japan with oil and other resources to support its war machine.

In September of 1940, Japan signed an agreement with both Germany and Italy. These three countries became known as the Axis powers. Japan was now joined with Germany and Italy against the Allies—Great Britain, France and the Soviet Union.

Japan was now ready to take over Southeast Asia, just as Hitler had already taken over most of Europe.

The United States had not yet entered the war in Europe. But it was supporting England and its defeated allies. And American diplomats were making every effort to force Japan to stop its military actions.

But the Japanese military forces rolled on.

Planning a Surprise

During the 1930s, there was little money in the United States to develop the military. The U.S. Army was smaller than the army of tiny Portugal. Even with increased military spending in 1940 and the start of the draft in September of that year, the U.S. armed forces were still small.

The military leaders of Japan knew this. But they also knew that American industry could build up a huge war machine quickly. So, in October 1941, the military and civilian leaders of Japan agreed that they would go to war against the United States.

General Hideki Tojo, Japan's prime minister, wanted to attack the Dutch and English colonies and the Philippines first. The Japanese navy, using submarines and aircraft, would attack the U.S. Pacific Fleet as it came to the rescue. However, Admiral Isoroku Yamamoto, commander in chief of the Japanese navy, disagreed with Tojo.

Yamamoto thought that a surprise attack on Pearl Harbor would cripple the U.S. Navy. Japan would then be free to conquer all of Southeast Asia. The island nations of Sumatra, Java, Borneo, New Guinea and the Philippines would quickly surrender.

Crewmen on a Japanese aircraft carrier cheer as a bomber rolls down the flight deck for takeoff.

Yamamoto won the argument. Tojo agreed that Japan would attack the United States at Pearl Harbor. Aircraft, pilots and ships were taken from the war in China. They were put in training for a secret mission. War with Japan was certain, but few Americans realized it.

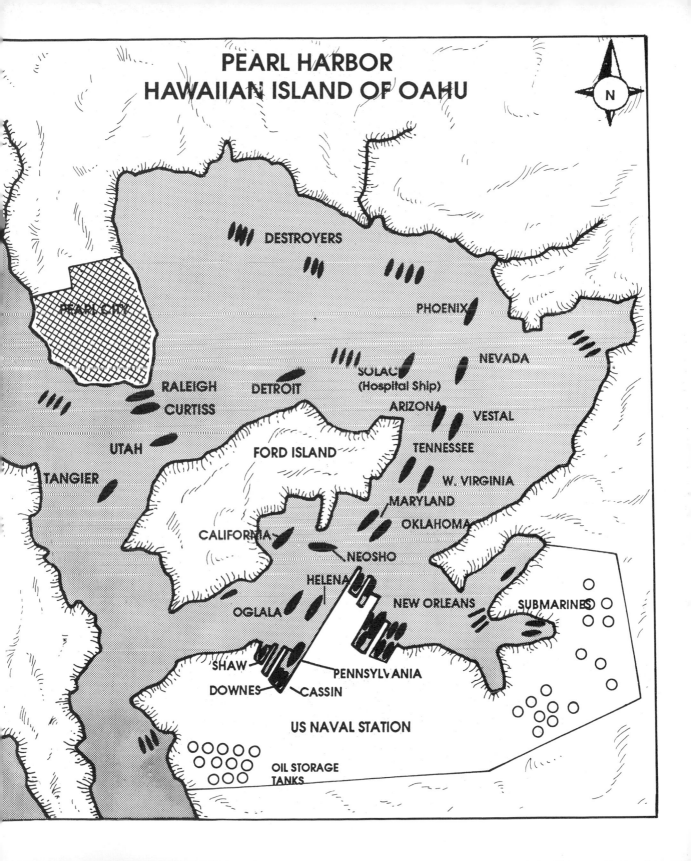

PEARL HARBOR
HAWAIIAN ISLAND OF OAHU

N

DESTROYERS

PEARL CITY

PHOENIX

NEVADA

RALEIGH   DETROIT   SOLACE
                          (Hospital Ship)

CURTISS   ARIZONA   VESTAL

UTAH   TENNESSEE

TANGIER   FORD ISLAND   W. VIRGINIA

                          MARYLAND

CALIFORNIA   OKLAHOMA

             NEOSHO

HELENA   SUBMARINES

OGLALA   NEW ORLEANS

SHAW   PENNSYLVANIA

DOWNES   CASSIN

US NAVAL STATION

OIL STORAGE
TANKS

Chapter 3

"EAST WIND, RAIN" THE JAPANESE ATTACK

On November 26, a force of over 30 Japanese warships left Japan to sail toward Hawaii. The final order for the Pearl Harbor raid was given on December 2.

The strike force sailed through the northern Pacific with six aircraft carriers in two columns of three. The flagship *Abukuma* and several destroyers were in the lead. One cruiser protected each side of the column. Two battleships and numerous supply vessels brought up the rear, while submarines scouted ahead, searching for U.S. patrols.

The Pilots and Their Training

More than 500 Japanese pilots and gunners were to take part in the Pearl Harbor aerial attack. They all had many hundreds of hours of combat experience in the war with China. They were the most skilled pilots in Japan. And they were enormously dedicated—they were ready to die for emperor and country.

A large harbor on the Japanese coast, Kagashima Bay, similar in size and shape to Pearl Harbor, had been used for training. The air crews had practiced bombing, gunnery and torpedo attacks against shiplike targets. The Japanese navy had even laid out a scale model of Pearl Harbor and the island of Oahu. It showed the locations of ships and other targets.

For years Japanese spies had been stationed in Hawaii.

They had learned all about U.S. military activities on the islands. In the months just before the raid, reports were made almost daily. As a result, the strike force commander, Vice Admiral Chuichi Nagumo, and his staff knew the exact location of every warship and every land target. American reporters even wrote of Japanese submarines being seen in the area. But no one paid any attention . . . until it was too late.

Attack Ordered

Up until the very last minute, the Pearl Harbor attack could have been canceled. The code words "East Wind, Rain" radioed to Admiral Nagumo told him to continue eastward. His strike force was to complete its mission and "rain" bombs on Pearl Harbor.

On the morning of December 7, 1941, Commander Mitsuo Fuchida was excited. He was the commander of the first wave of aircraft that would take off from the Japanese aircraft carriers. At 6:15 A M he left with 183 other aircraft following in close formation.

As his huge force flew southward, Commander Fuchida

Vice Admiral Chuichi Nagumo, commander of the Japanese strike force that attacked Pearl Harbor

"Zeke" fighter aircraft preparing to take off from a Japanese aircraft carrier to attack Pearl Harbor

kept a close watch for American aerial or naval patrols. If discovered, the attackers might have to turn back. However, he saw nothing. The warning from the two U.S. radar operators had been ignored.

Under partly cloudy skies, Commander Fuchida used his radio direction finder to home in on Honolulu radio stations. Several float planes from the strike force had flown ahead and radioed back that all was quiet. They also reported that the U.S. fleet was in the harbor.

As his huge wave of fighters and bombers swept over the island of Oahu, Fuchida could see his target clearly in the early morning light. He shouted into his radio, "Tora! Tora! Tora!" These code words meant that the attack had begun.

A Japanese "Val" dive-bomber in action. It is preparing to dive toward its target.

The Attack

Fuchida fired several Black Dragon flares as a signal to attack. At 7:55 A.M. he led his squadrons across Pearl Harbor. Bombs fell and exploded. Torpedoes tore through the water and dive-bombers screamed to the attack.

On the ground, all of the island of Oahu was rudely awakened. The word went out at once: *"Air raid, Pearl Harbor! This is no drill!"*

Commander Fuchida's bombers aimed at the battleships lined up at Ford Island. They struck with terrible effect, raining death and destruction on every target. Other bombers and fighter aircraft strafed and bombed Wheeler, Hickam, Ewa and Kaneohe air bases. The main U.S. Air Corps, Navy and Marine Corps aviation squadrons were stationed at these fields. The attackers zoomed over the navy yard and other bases on Oahu and Ford Island. They were all badly damaged.

At almost the same moment, Lieutenant Commander Shigeharu Murata led his torpedo planes to the southern end of the island. Sweeping in at wave-top level, they released their torpedoes. Seven giant battleships received one or more direct hits. In addition, all ships were attacked by high-flying bombers. Giant explosions tore the American ships apart.

"Zero" fighters protected the attackers from above. When it was clear that no American aircraft were going to take off, the Zeros began strafing attacks on the airfields.

More damage was done to the already blazing aircraft, hangars and barracks.

After using up all of their bombs and ammunition, Commander Fuchida's victorious squadrons flew back to their carriers.

One hour later, Commander Shigekazu Shimazaki led another wave of 181 aircraft in a follow-up attack. They added to the damage done by the first wave. But this time they were met with gunfire from U.S. forces. After the shock of the first attack, anti-aircraft guns began to fill the air with flak. Several P-40 fighters were able to take off to meet the attackers.

At 9:45 A.M. the Japanese attack ended. First reports showed that of the nearly 400 U.S. aircraft stationed on Oahu airfields most were destroyed or damaged. Only a few were still able to fly.

U.S. Navy ships and shipyards burning at Pearl Harbor. Anti-aircraft gun crews had finally begun to fight back.

This captured Japanese photograph was taken during the Pearl Harbor attack. The U.S. battleships neatly lined up next to Ford Island made perfect targets for the bombers.

The Tally

The Japanese aircraft, out of ammunition and running short on fuel, headed north. One after the other they landed on their aircraft carriers.

Commander Fuchida had been the first to take off. But he was one of the last to return. Reporting to Admiral Nagumo, Fuchida urged that aircraft be quickly rearmed and refueled to attack again.

Admiral Nagumo had not been in favor of attacking Pearl Harbor in the first place. He decided that the risks of making another attack were too great. Japan's main targets, the U.S. aircraft carriers, had not been at Pearl Harbor and had therefore escaped damage. These aircraft carriers, the

Supplies of ammunition explode in a spectacular display as the destroyer USS Shaw receives a direct hit by a Japanese bomb.

USS *Lexington* and the USS *Enterprise,* were at sea, delivering aircraft to Wake and Midway islands. They might appear on the horizon at any minute!

With a great victory to his credit, at 1:30 P.M., Admiral Nagumo ordered the Pearl Harbor strike force to return to Japan. Part of the fleet later broke away and on December 21 attacked and helped occupy Wake island, 2,000 miles to the west of Hawaii.

Of the 392 Japanese aircraft that had taken off in the two attacking waves, 324 had returned to their carriers. A number had been lost in takeoff or landing. Others had been shot down by U.S. aircraft or anti-aircraft fire. One Japanese squadron leader had deliberately crashed his burning plane into a hangar at an airfield. Such an action was known as a kamikaze, or "divine wind," suicide attack.

In addition to the Japanese midget subs attacked earlier that day, two more had entered the harbor to launch their torpedoes at close range. One was sunk by the destroyer USS *Monoghan.* Another was forced ashore and one crew member was captured. He became the first Japanese prisoner of war.

One Japanese pilot crash-landed on a distant island in the Hawaiian group several hours after the attack. The island had only 200 inhabitants and no radio. They had not heard about the attack on Pearl Harbor. They took the strange invader prisoner.

The Japanese attack on Pearl Harbor was over in only one hour and forty-five minutes. Much of the U. S. Pacific Fleet was ruined. Hundreds of aircraft and buildings and tons of supplies were in flames. Several thousand young Americans were killed, missing or wounded. Except for the fact that the U.S. aircraft carriers were not in the harbor, the Japanese had succeeded in their mission.

Japan officially declared war on the United States at 11:40 A.M., December 7, 1941 (December 8, Tokyo time), four hours after the attack on Pearl Harbor had started.

Chapter 4

DESTRUCTION AND DEATH AT PEARL HARBOR

Only a few men aboard the American ships anchored in the harbor were awake and on duty as the attack started. Most crews were either onshore or asleep in their bunks. After the first shock, officers and men, no matter what their rank or experience, fought back in any way they could.

Onshore, ammunition stores were locked up. At first many guns wouldn't work because trained crews were not there. Gradually machine guns began to fire back at the raiders. Fire-fighting crews went to work.

Roaring in over Pearl City, the main city on the harbor, Japanese torpedo-bombers first attacked the battleship *Utah* and the cruisers *Detroit* and *Raleigh*. The *Utah* took

---

The Japanese attack on land bases near Pearl Harbor destroyed more than 80 navy planes.

two hits and immediately began to sink, while the *Raleigh* was hit by one torpedo. One of this group of torpedo-bombers held its fire. It zoomed across Ford Island to attack the minelayer *Oglala* and the light cruiser *Helena*. Missing the *Oglala*, the torpedo sank the *Helena*, right next to it. The *Oglala* was destroyed by the force of the explosions on the *Helena*.

Death of the Battleships

The south side of Ford Island was "Battleship Row." Except for aircraft carriers, these heavily armed ships were the biggest vessels in the U.S. Navy. A second wave of Japanese planes roared in from the south and released their torpedoes. Five of the seven battleships at Ford Island received one or more torpedo strikes. The *Oklahoma, Tennessee, West Virginia, Arizona* and *Nevada* were burst open by torpedo explosions.

The USS Maryland, *seen here burning and sinking, was one of the U.S. battleships hit during the Pearl Harbor raid.*

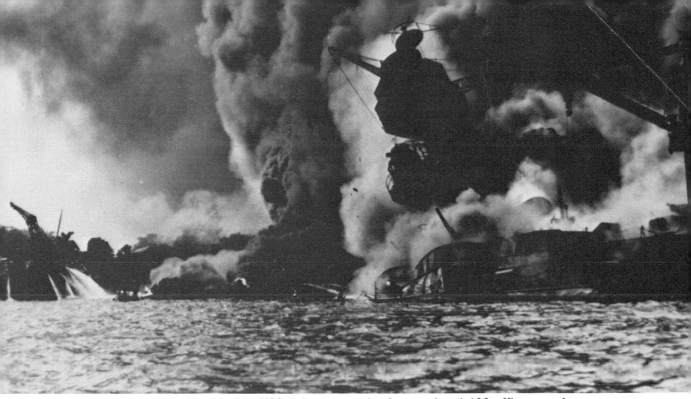

The burning battleship USS Arizona *capsized, trapping 1,103 officers and men in a permanent underwater grave.*

Meanwhile, high above, Commander Fuchida's Nakajima "Kate" bombers were unloading their deadly cargo. Thousand-pound armor-piercing bombs struck the ships below. The deadly bombs exploded deep inside their targets, which had already been made helpless by the torpedoes.

One bomb struck far into the front turrets of the *Arizona,* causing ammunition to explode. Five or six more bombs hit the already dying ship, making it roll over. Almost all of its helpless crew members were trapped as the ship sank. At that moment, 1,103 officers and men died on the battleship *Arizona.* Only a few hundred survived.

After the shock of the first attacks had passed, the crews of all ships still afloat manned their guns. With shipmates dying all around them, heroic men began to fight back. Every person who could handle a gun or pass the ammunition went to work. A navy chaplain inspired a popular version of the song "Praise the Lord and Pass the Ammunition." He, too, joined the ranks and passed ammunition to an anti-aircraft gun crew.

Crackling flames, exploding bombs and ammunition, and the shouts of rescue crews filled the air. The great Pacific Fleet of the U.S. Navy was battered, and dozens of mighty ships were sinking. Even so, the defenders, fighting with too little and too late, did some damage to the enemy. The anti-aircraft fire and the few fighter aircraft that managed to take off slowed the second wave of attackers. But little could be done except to rescue the wounded, control the damage, and hope for the attack to end.

The *Nevada,* even though badly damaged, was the only battleship able to get up steam and head toward the open sea. Japanese planes continued to attack the battered ship as it moved toward the harbor entrance. Its captain bravely ordered his ship to be run aground inside the harbor. If the *Nevada* had been sunk in the harbor entrance, Pearl Harbor would have been unusable for months.

The air force bases at Wheeler and Hickam fields were also badly hit. Here, a destroyed P-40 and other planes lie in front of a damaged hangar.

Sailors at the Naval Air Station continued to search the skies for enemy raiders after the Japanese attack on Pearl Harbor.

The second attack wave of Japanese planes was less deadly than the first, but it still caused a lot of destruction. The battleship *Pennsylvania,* in dry dock along with two destroyers, the *Cassin* and the *Downes*, received severe bomb damage.

Destruction on Land

Onshore, the damage was no less dramatic. Everything was in chaos. Awakened out of sound sleep, soldiers at Schofield Barracks, the main army base, rushed to their guns. Airmen at the air corps and marine corps bases ran for their planes.

Within the first minutes of battle, nearly half of the combat aircraft on the island were destroyed. Almost every air base on the island was filled with burning and exploding planes and hangars.

Men of every rank sprang into action. Ammunition was dragged out of storerooms. Machine-gun nests and anti-aircraft stations were quickly manned. Many soldiers and sailors, armed only with pistols and rifles, fired back at the airborne attackers.

Three civilians were killed in this bullet-riddled car in a residential district eight miles from Pearl Harbor.

Pilots scrambled toward their aircraft only to find many with guns unloaded and not ready for takeoff. Most were damaged or in flames. A few aircraft did get into the air.

Air Corps Lieutenants Kenneth Taylor and George Welch jumped into their P-40s and were able to take off and attack the invaders. Between them, they shot down seven of the attacking Japanese aircraft.

A flight of twelve B-17s, coming in from California, arrived during the battle. Unfortunately, their guns were stowed away and not ready for use. They were low on fuel. They had to land. Fortunately, only one was shot down by the attackers. The others made safe landings at smaller airstrips on the island.

Even navy fighters returning from the aircraft carrier USS *Enterprise* entered the battle. Nine of them were shot down. A few of those nine were shot down by American gunners on the ground. They had panicked and shot at anything they saw in the air.

The naval base on Ford Island, where the Catalina PBY patrol bombers were stationed, was another complete disaster. Lined up onshore or floating in the water, more than a dozen of these great flying boats were destroyed.

Above—B-17 bombers parked on airfields were bombed and strafed.
Not one was able to take off to avoid the attackers or to search for the
Japanese strike force.

Below—The destroyers Cassin and Downes were wrecked as they lay in
dry dock for repair. The battleship Pennsylvania, only slightly damaged,
can be seen behind them.

Watching in Horror

In only one hour and forty-five minutes, the attackers left a scene of death and destruction. Many ships of the United States Pacific Fleet were sunk or damaged. Hundreds of aircraft and shore installations were in flames. In addition to 2,343 army, navy and marine corps personnel killed, 960 were missing and over 1,200 were wounded. When the final count of aircraft was made, of the 394 operational aircraft on the island, 188 of the army and navy aircraft had been destroyed and over 150 were severely damaged.

The fires on the military bases and on the damaged ships continued to burn for days. Hundreds of men were trapped inside sunken ships. Rescue efforts went on night and day until all hope was gone. There were countless acts of heroism by both civilian workers and military men and women. Side by side they rescued the injured and fought the flames and lessened the battle damage.

Salvage and repair work was started at once. Yes, there were many sunken and damaged ships and destroyed aircraft. But within just a few days, the U.S. Navy, Army and Army Air Corps were ready for action again.

This sailor killed during the Japanese attack on Pearl Harbor was only one among the 2,343 service men and women who died on December 7, 1941.

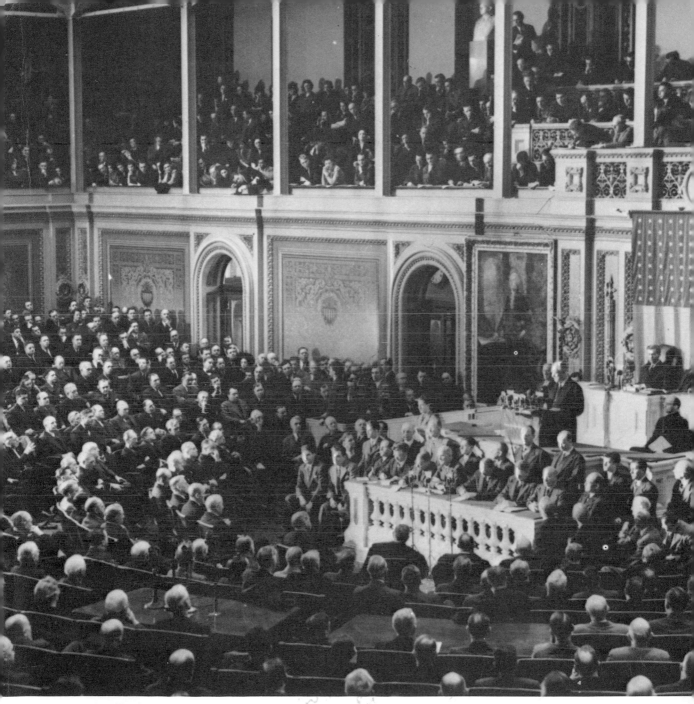

On December 8, 1941, President Franklin D. Roosevelt called a joint
session of Congress to officially declare war on Japan for its "unprovoked
and dastardly attack."

Chapter 5

"REMEMBER PEARL HARBOR!"

From the moment the news of the attack on Pearl Harbor became known in the United States, the attitude of most Americans changed. Before, they had figured that the war in Europe had nothing to do with them. They were also certain that the Japanese people wouldn't have the nerve to tackle the big and powerful United States.

But on Sunday afternoon, December 7, Americans began to shout, "Remember Pearl Harbor!" Suddenly, without warning, they were ready to go to war.

A battleship sinks at its dock as smoke from other burning ships fills the sky. Even at the moment of defeat, the United States flag flew bravely at Pearl Harbor.

Overnight, all anti-war feeling was wiped out. The American people, the United States government, the U.S. armed forces, and all of the power of American industry were bound together. Their only goal—victory over the Japanese and their allies, Germany and Italy!

Sadly, many Americans also began to look at Japanese-Americans with new eyes. They began to distrust even those Japanese-Americans whose families had been here for generations. They thought of them as possible enemies. Most Japanese had been in the United States for many years and were loyal American citizens. Within only a few weeks, plans were being made to send all Japanese-Americans to camps where most of them would have to live until the war was over.

The Cost of the Attack

The Japanese attack was a great blow to American pride. Admiral Chester W. Nimitz, who would command the Pacific naval forces for most of the war, said that the Japanese made one mistake that day. They attacked only once. A second and even a third attack on Pearl Harbor that day would truly have wiped out U.S. naval power in the Pacific.

It was a sad day in American history when Japanese-Americans were sent to special camps where they were forced to live while the war lasted. The government feared that they might spy for Japan or commit acts of sabotage.

A permanent memorial was built on top of the capsized USS Arizona.

But the U.S. losses were not as great as they seemed at first. Eight battleships were lost or damaged during the raid, but the war was not going to be won by battleships. It was going to be fought and won in the air. The dozen additional ships lost were not important, and replacements were already being built.

The most important fact was that no U.S. Navy aircraft carriers were lost. New ones would have cost millions of dollars and taken several years to build. By that time, the U.S. would probably have lost the war.

The memory of the men who died and fought against the Japanese that day will live forever. Most of them died on the ships that were bombed and sunk in the harbor. A monument has been built on the flooded hull of the battleship USS *Arizona* just where it sank. Each year, hundreds of thousands of visitors to Hawaii pay their respects to those who died at Pearl Harbor.

The 2,400 lives lost that day could never be replaced. But 8 million other American men and women would join ranks to avenge the defeat at Pearl Harbor. The 19 ships and the several hundred aircraft lost that day would be replaced by tens of thousands as the vast power of American industry went to work.

Furthermore, many important targets were not harmed. The gasoline storage tanks, ammunition dumps, naval repair shops, dry docks and other facilities around the harbor were undamaged. The cleanup and repair job was started immediately. Much of Pearl Harbor was operating as usual the very next day.

The United States Declares War

On Monday, December 8, the president of the United States, Franklin D. Roosevelt, called together the nation's senators and congressmen. He asked them to declare war on Japan for an "unprovoked and dastardly attack." Most Americans wanted to declare war on Germany and Italy also. Roosevelt did not. There had been no direct attack on the United States by those two nations.

However, the problem was solved when Adolf Hitler of Germany and Benito Mussolini of Italy both declared war on the United States a few days later. Great Britain had declared war on Japan even before the United States had. The United States, Great Britain and Allied governments that had escaped to England were now at war with Germany, Italy and Japan.

Plans were being made to fight the war the United States had not wanted. Admiral Husband E. Kimmel and Lieutenant General Walter C. Short, the navy and army commanders in Hawaii, were both removed from their commands. Admiral Chester W. Nimitz, General Dwight D. Eisenhower, General Douglas MacArthur, Admiral W. F. "Bull" Halsey and other great leaders stepped forward to take charge.

Japan Spreads the Attack

It turned out that Pearl Harbor was only one of the targets Japan was aiming for that day. Other Japanese task forces and fleets had spread out through the Pacific to try to take over more of Southeast Asia.

Later on the morning of December 7 (December 8, Tokyo time), 2,000 miles to the west, other Japanese aircraft bombed Wake island. It was invaded several days later and surrendered to the Japanese. Destroyers from the Pearl Harbor strike force also shelled Midway island. The island of Guam was taken on December 10. All three of these islands were American possessions.

Singapore, at the southern tip of the Malay peninsula, was Great Britain's strongest base in the Far East. Without warning, bombs fell on that city early on the morning of

Attacked at the same time as Pearl Harbor, Wake island surrendered to the Japanese a few days later.

The pride of the Royal Navy's Asiatic fleet, the HMS Prince of Wales *and* HMS Repulse, *were both sunk by Japanese bombers.*

December 8. Reports were received of an approaching invasion fleet. The British warships HMS *Prince of Wales* and HMS *Repulse*, known as Force Z, set sail that afternoon to fight the invaders landing in the north. This turned out to be the wrong decision on the part of the British naval commanders.

On December 9, Force Z was spotted by a Japanese submarine. It alerted other forces. At 11:00 A.M. the next morning, long-range Japanese torpedo-bombers swept in from bases in Thailand and Indochina.

The two warships tried to avoid the attackers, but without any air protection they were easy targets. Both the *Repulse* and *Prince of Wales* were struck by at least a half dozen torpedoes. They both sank immediately, with a loss of more than 800 lives.

Following the great victory at Pearl Harbor and now the defeat of Force Z, the Japanese were in control of the eastern Pacific Ocean from Hawaii to the Malay peninsula. At the same time, the Japanese landed in Thailand, Malaya and on key islands. Tarawa, Makin and other islands in the Gilbert group northeast of Australia were bombed and occupied. So were the Philippines.

One after the other, English, Dutch and American bases in the southeast Pacific and on the Asian mainland were overcome. Hong Kong, Singapore and the Dutch islands of Indonesia all fell. The stage was set for the Japanese to occupy all of Southeast Asia and most of the key islands of the Pacific.

The battle that would rage for almost four long years was under way. December 7, 1941, at Pearl Harbor was only the tragic beginning for the United States.

Hundreds of thousands of people all over the islands and mainland of Asia were being taken prisoner by the Japanese. Many of them would die in captivity. Children would be born in Japanese prison camps and would not know freedom until 1945.

It would be a long, hard struggle to stop the Japanese from capturing the lands and peoples of Asia. But millions of Americans were willing to fight and risk their lives for freedom.

"Farewell to Thee"—In a traditional Hawaiian ceremony, sailors paid tribute in the spring of 1942 to comrades who fell at Pearl Harbor.

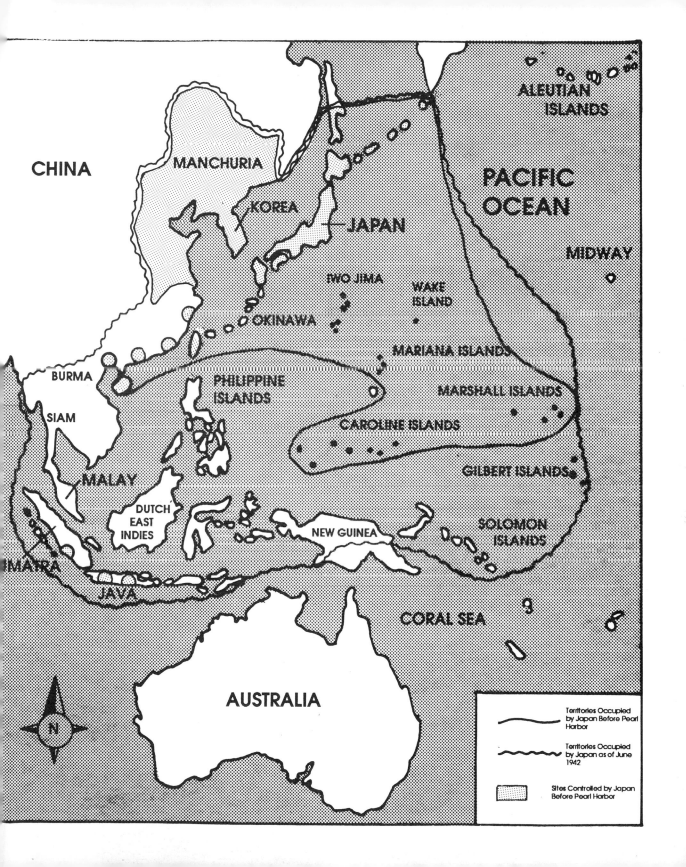

CHINA

MANCHURIA

KOREA

JAPAN

BURMA

SIAM

MALAY

DUTCH
EAST
INDIES

SUMATRA

JAVA

AUSTRALIA

PACIFIC
OCEAN

ALEUTIAN
ISLANDS

MIDWAY

IWO JIMA

WAKE
ISLAND

OKINAWA

MARIANA ISLANDS

PHILIPPINE
ISLANDS

MARSHALL ISLANDS

CAROLINE ISLANDS

GILBERT ISLANDS

NEW GUINEA

SOLOMON
ISLANDS

CORAL SEA

N

Territories Occupied
by Japan Before Pearl
Harbor

Territories Occupied
by Japan as of June
1942

Sites Controlled by Japan
Before Pearl Harbor

A Closer Look at . . .

THE JAPANESE STRIKE FORCE

Japanese Aircraft Carriers made up the main strength of the strike force. Shown here *(left)* is the *Akagi*, one of the six carriers to take part in the Pearl Harbor raid. Each carrier was able to launch 60 to 70 aircraft.

Japanese Battleships—Battleships, cruisers, destroyers, submarines, and assorted supply ships and tankers made up the rest of the strike force. Shown here *(right)* is the battleship *Kirishima*.

Mitsubishi A6M2 "Zeke" *(left)*—This Japanese fighter, an early version of the famed "Zero," flew top cover for the bombers and then machine-gunned ground targets during the attack on Pearl Harbor. A single-seat, single-engine, low-wing navy fighter, it was armed with forward-firing machine guns or 20mm cannon.

Nakajima B5N2 "Kate" *(right)*—This two-seat, single-engine, low-wing aircraft was used mainly as a torpedo-bomber. Flying at low levels over water, it could drop a 2,000-pound propeller-driven torpedo aimed directly at enemy surface vessels. It carried both forward- and rear-firing machine guns and could also be used in conventional bombing attacks.

PEARL HARBOR DAMAGE REPORT

"Battleship Row"—The U.S. Navy had one of the finest fleets of battleships in the world. Eight of these giant ships were in Pearl Harbor on December 7, 1941. Seven of the giant ships were hit on the first attack. The battleships *Utah*, *Maryland*, *Oklahoma*, *Tennessee*, *West Virginia*, *Arizona* and *Nevada* were all torpedoed by the first wave of attackers. The USS *California (left)* was bombed at Ford Island.

Aircraft Carriers—The Japanese had hoped to find the two giant aircraft carriers, the USS *Lexington* and the USS *Enterprise (right)*, at Pearl Harbor. Luckily they were at sea after delivering aircraft to other island bases.

Army and navy aircraft destroyed—Of the 394 operational aircraft at the air bases on the island, 188 were destroyed and over 150 were damaged *(left)*. Only a few P-40s were able to take off and attack the enemy. Navy fighters returning from aircraft carriers also entered the battle, only to be shot down.

Navy and air corps bases attacked—In addition to attacking the ships in the harbor, the Japanese planes strafed and bombed navy installations, air corps fields and army bases. Shown here *(right)* are hangars and aircraft in ruins.

GLOSSARY

aircraft carrier A large, flat-topped ship on which aircraft take off and land.

airstrip Any smooth runway or landing surface.

Allies The countries that opposed Germany, Italy and Japan in World War II: Great Britain, the United States, the Soviet Union and France.

ammunition Bullets, artillery shells, or rockets.

anti-aircraft Large cannon or machine guns used to shoot at attacking aircraft.

armament Any military weapons.

artillery Large weapons such as cannon, howitzers and missile launchers suitably mounted and fired by a crew.

Axis The partnership of Germany, Italy and Japan.

battleship The largest modern warship.

cover Protection. Fighter aircraft fly cover for bombers.

cruiser A high-speed warship, next in size to a battleship.

depression A time of poor business and unemployment.

depth charge A device that explodes underwater.

destroyer A fast, small warship armed with guns, torpedoes and depth charges.

dive-bomber A plane that aims its bombs by diving.

dry dock A large fixed or floating enclosure from which water is pumped in or out; used for repairing ships.

flak Exploding anti-aircraft shells.

float planes Aircraft that can operate from water.

fuselage The main body of an airplane.

radar Radio equipment that detects airplanes and ships and determines their distance, speed and altitude. Short for RAdio Detection And Ranging.

radio direction finder A radio device used on aircraft or ships to determine direction to another station.

sabotage A destructive act by enemy agents.

shrapnel Pieces of metal from exploding shells.

strafe To fire machine guns at ground targets from low-flying aircraft.

torpedo A self-propelled underwater missile that explodes on impact with a target.

torpedo-bombers Aircraft equipped to carry and launch torpedoes.

turret A rotating armored enclosure for guns and gun crews on naval vessels, tanks or aircraft.

INDEX